BEGINNING

SIGN LANGUAGE

SERIES

Can I Help?

Helping the hearing impaired in emergency situations.

by S. Harold Collins

Illustrated by Kathy Kifer, Dahna Solar and Dan Gilmore

Published by

Garlic Press

100 Hillview Lane #2
Eugene, OR 97401

ISBN 0-931993-57-1
Order Number GP-057

Introduction

What can you do to assist a hearing impaired person who is in need of help? —who might be injured? —or who might need medical help? **Can I Help?** is organized to prepare you to assist a hearing impaired person in need of help. Suggestions, signs, and vocabulary are organized in the following way:

A Quick Reference Guide and Vocabulary Index allow immediate access to signs.

You may find yourself needing to help a person who is hearing impaired. What should you do? How should you act?

Here are some helpful suggestions:

1. Let the person know that you have some signing skills.

2. Let the person know that you are there to help and that you will do your best.

3. For older children and adults, you can always write a message in addition to your signing.

4. For younger children, you may have to pantomime or act out your message.

Remember that for small children, it is often difficult for them to tell you what is wrong. Be patient. Be as visual as possible—that means use gestures, draw, act out.

Can I help?

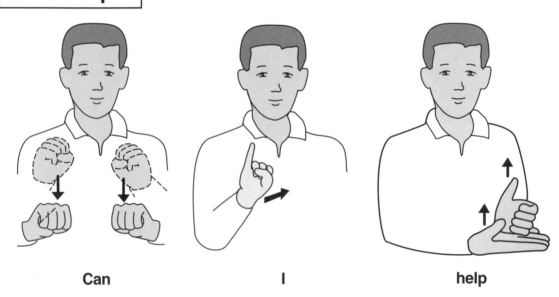

| Can | I | help |

Notice that we did not use a sign for the question mark (?). You can trace a question mark in the air with your index finger if you wish. We have chosen not to show that here.

Many signs make use of letters of the alphabet, such as "I" shown above and "OK" on the next page. Some signs use the first letter of the word in combination with a movement. The complete finger alphabet is shown on the inside front cover of this book.

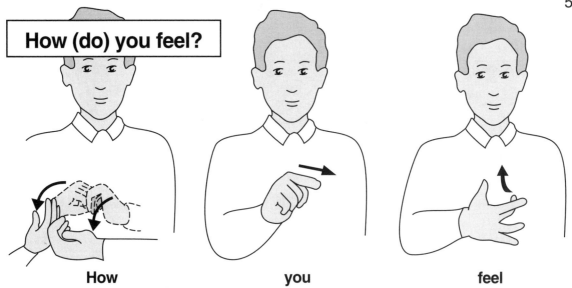

How (do) you feel?

How   you   feel

Notice that we have not used a sign for "do". In more formal Signed English, signers will use a sign for "do". But our idea is still understood without signing "do". Other words that will not be signed in this book will also be placed in parentheses.

sick   dizzy   confused

hurt   OK

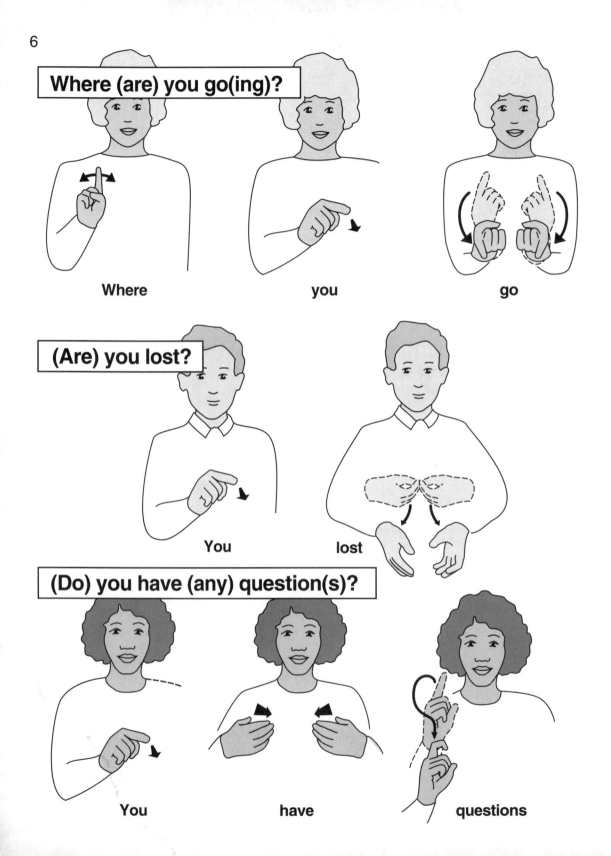

Where (are) you go(ing)?

Where

you

go

(Are) you lost?

You

lost

(Do) you have (any) question(s)?

You

have

questions

Emergency situations require important decisions. An emergency situation might involve an injury, an illness, a fire, or an accident.

An emergency often means that you must not only help a person but also get additional help for that person.

What should you do in an emergency situation? Here are some suggestions:
1. Let the person know that you are there to help *and* that you will get additional help.
2. Get additional help:
   • Ask for help.
   • Call **911** or dial **Operator** to ask for help. State that a person is hearing impaired and that they will need an interpreter (An interpreter is a person who is an excellent signer.)

I know a little bit (of) sign language.

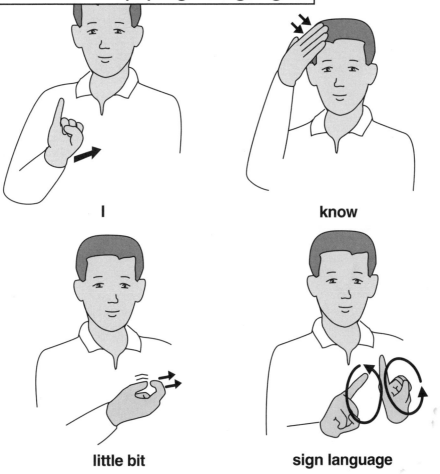

I

know

little bit

sign language

I (will) try (to) help.

I   try   help

This (is an) emergency.

This   emergency

(Do) you need help?

You   need   help

accident

danger

police

fire

fire truck

interpreter

Suppose you need to help a hearing impaired person by making a phone call. And suppose that the person you must contact is also hearing impaired. How do you talk by phone to a hearing impaired person? You talk with the help of a **relay service.**

The law requires each state to have a relay service. A relay person at the service you call types your words into a device known as a **TDD**. Most hearing impaired people have a TDD. The TDD is like a telephone-typewritrer which has a screen to display typed messages. Using the TDD, the relay person calls the person you want and types your message to them. That person then types back to the relay person, and the relay person reads the response to you.

To get the number of your local relay service, use your phone book or dial **0** and ask the operator.

Who (do) you want me (to) telephone?

Who   **you**   **want**

me   **telephone**

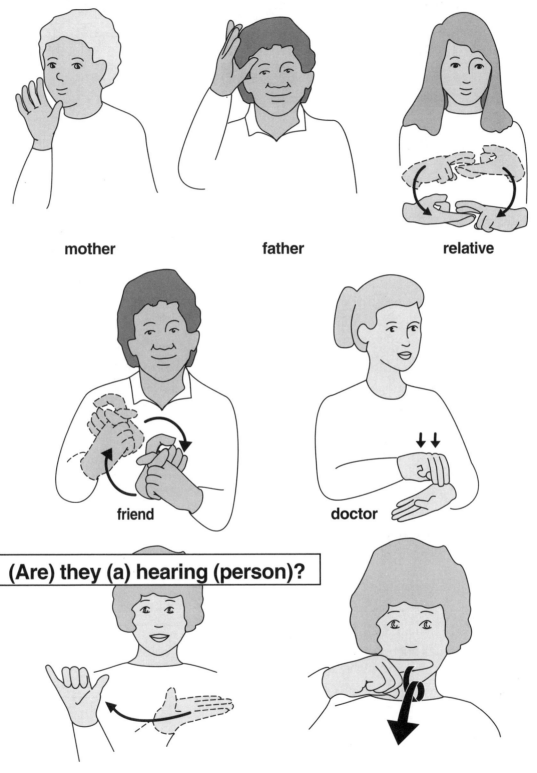

mother father relative

friend doctor

(Are) they (a) hearing (person)?

They hearing

What (is) your telephone number? address?

What   your   telephone

number   address

Proper names such as addresses can be spelled. See inside the front cover for the finger alphabet and the inside back cover for numbers.

Giving directions is often necessary to help someone.

Directions should be short and to the point. This is very important in an emergency situation where someone is hurt or sick.

Directions should be reassuring. You need to let the person know what you are doing. They must understand that you are there to help them.

(It's) important (to) follow directions.

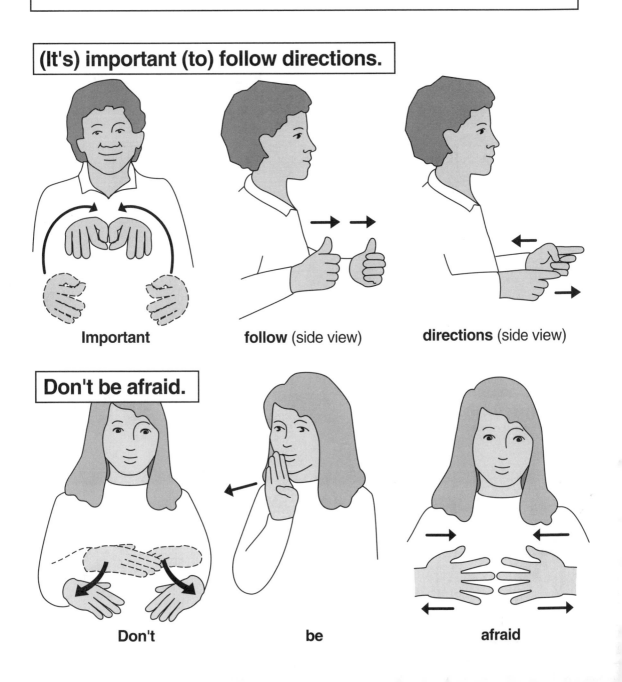

Important

follow (side view)

directions (side view)

Don't be afraid.

Don't

be

afraid

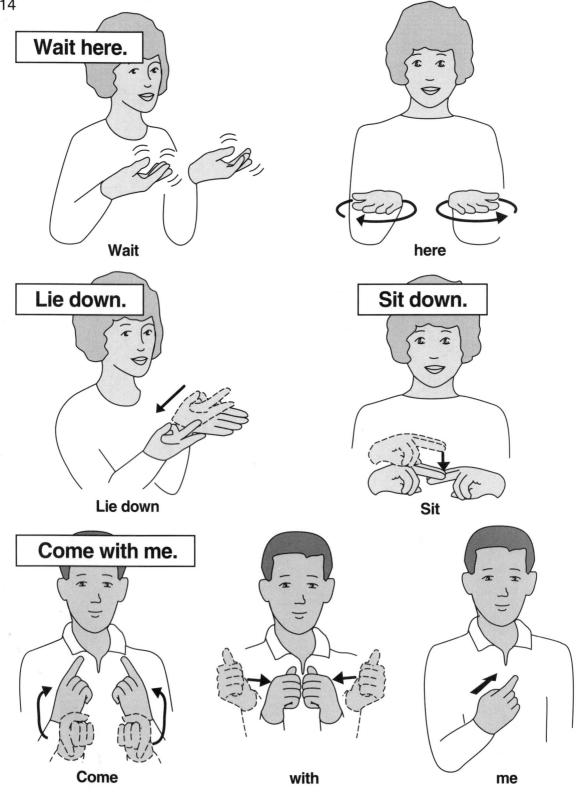

Wait here.

Wait

here

Lie down.

Lie down

Sit down.

Sit

Come with me.

Come

with

me

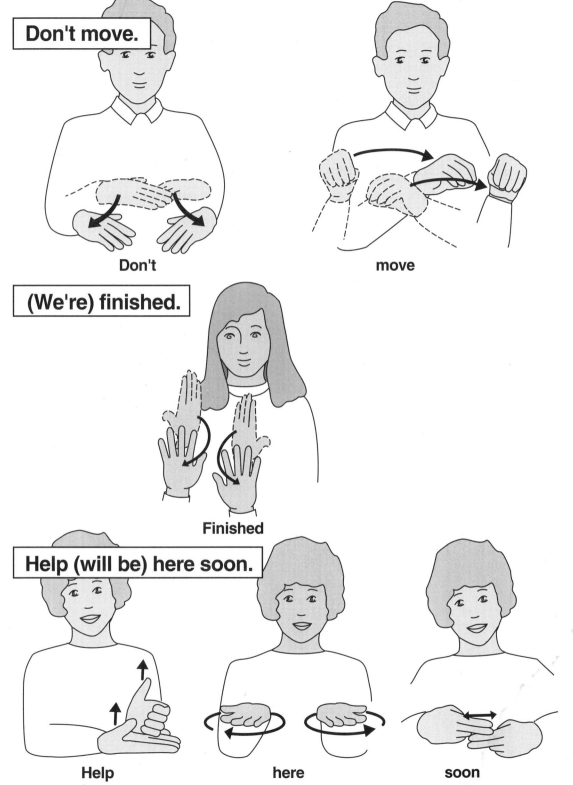

Don't move.

Don't

move

(We're) finished.

Finished

Help (will be) here soon.

Help

here

soon

Medical Help

You may need to help someone who is hurt or sick. You may need to use all the helpful suggestions that you have already learned.

An Interpreter is very important when someone needs medical help. When an interpreter is not available, message writing is helpful.

Remember, if you don't have medical training you can't act as a doctor or a nurse. You can best help in medical situations by giving comfort to an injured person and by contacting medical help—a doctor, nurse or interpreter.

How long (have) you (been) sick?

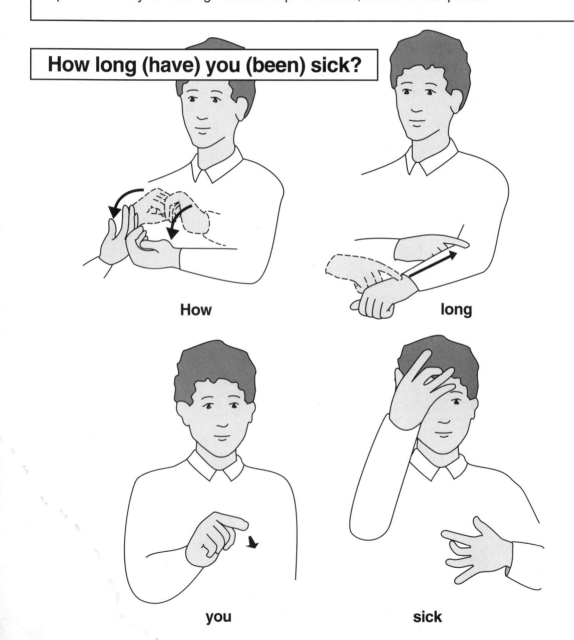

How

long

you

sick

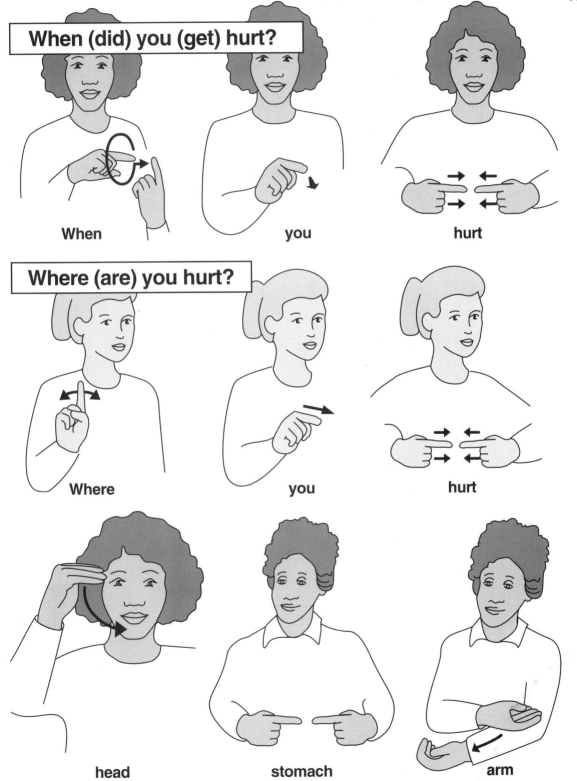

When (did) you (get) hurt?

When   **you**   **hurt**

Where (are) you hurt?

Where   **you**   **hurt**

head   **stomach**   **arm**

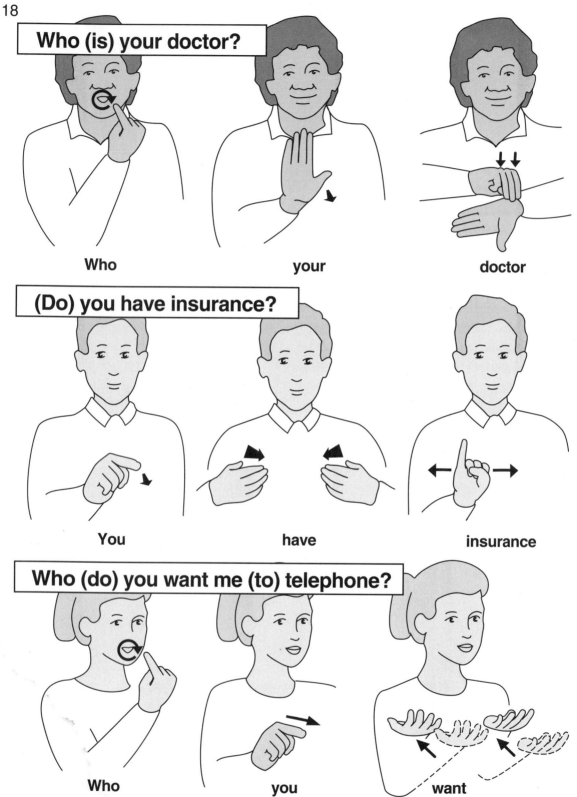

Who (is) your doctor?

Who   your   doctor

(Do) you have insurance?

You   have   insurance

Who (do) you want me (to) telephone?

Who   you   want

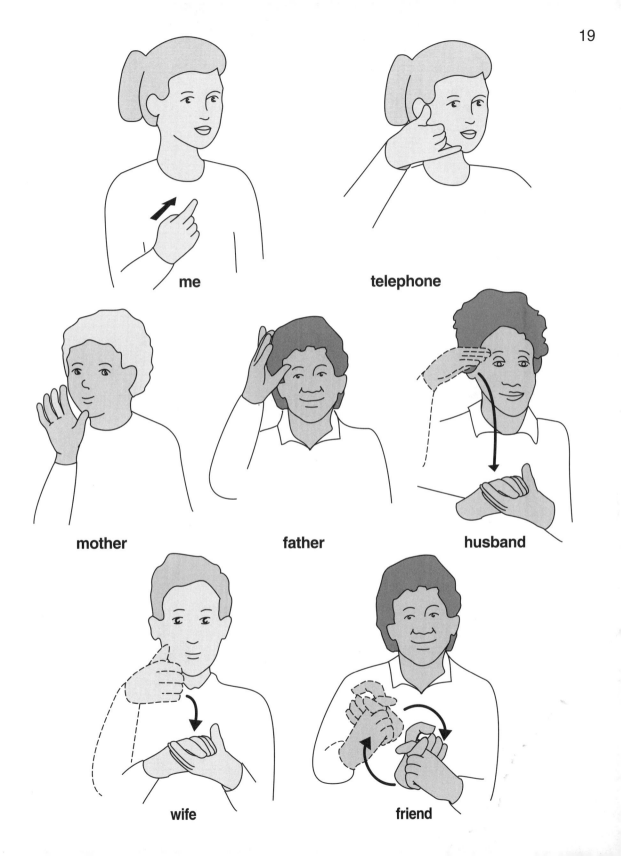

me

telephone

mother

father

husband

wife

friend

Additional Medical Signs

medicine

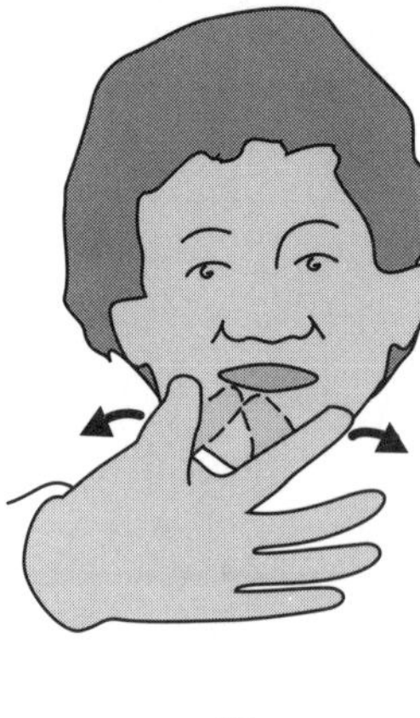

pill

shot

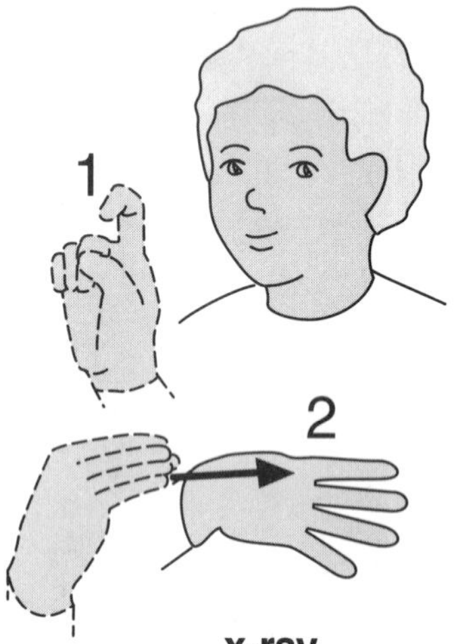

x-ray

operation

cast

fever

hospital

ambulance

nurse

blood

examination

poison

nauseous

breathe

doctor

heart attack

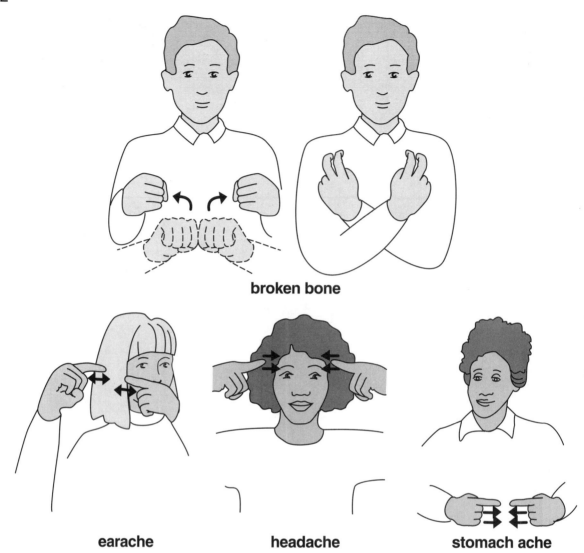

broken bone

earache   **headache**   **stomach ache**

QUICK REFERENCE

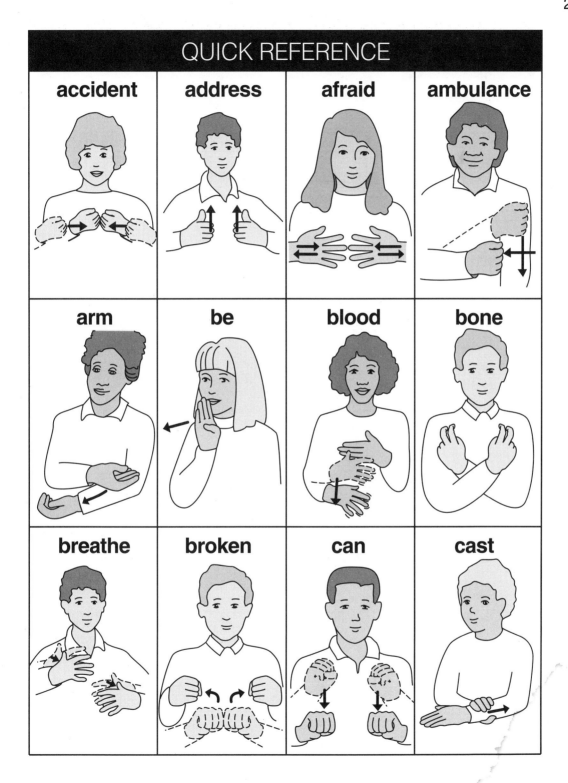

accident	address	afraid	ambulance
arm	**be**	**blood**	**bone**
breathe	**broken**	**can**	**cast**

QUICK REFERENCE

come	**confused**	**danger**	**directions**
dizzy	**doctor**	**don't**	**earache**
emergency	**examination**	**father**	**feel**

QUICK REFERENCE

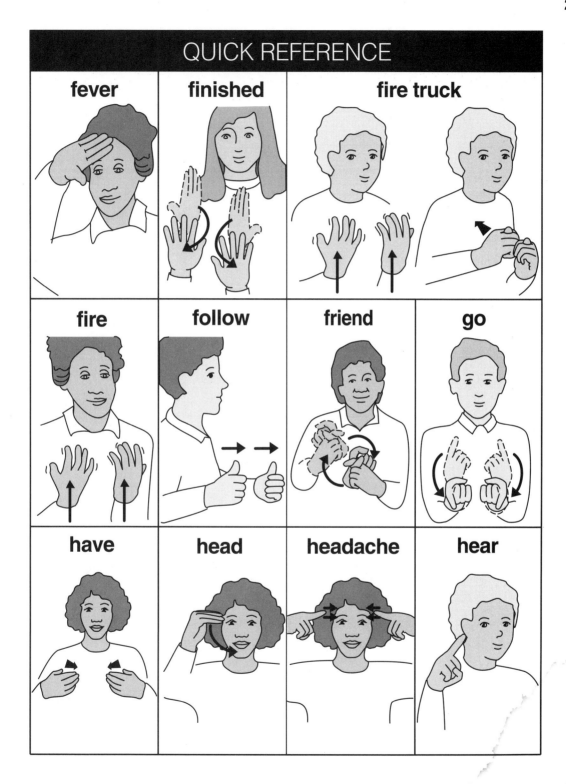

fever	finished	fire truck
fire	**follow**	**friend**
have	**head**	**headache**

go

hear

QUICK REFERENCE

hearing	heart attack	help	here
hospital	how	hurt	husband
I	important	interpreter	

QUICK REFERENCE

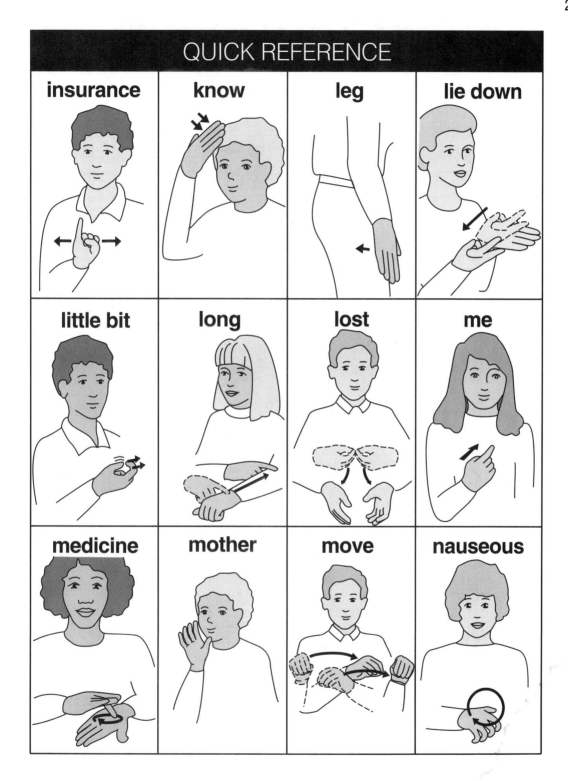

insurance	know	leg	lie down
little bit	long	lost	me
medicine	mother	move	nauseous

QUICK REFERENCE

need	number	nurse	OK
operation	pill	poison	police
questions	relative	shot	sick

QUICK REFERENCE

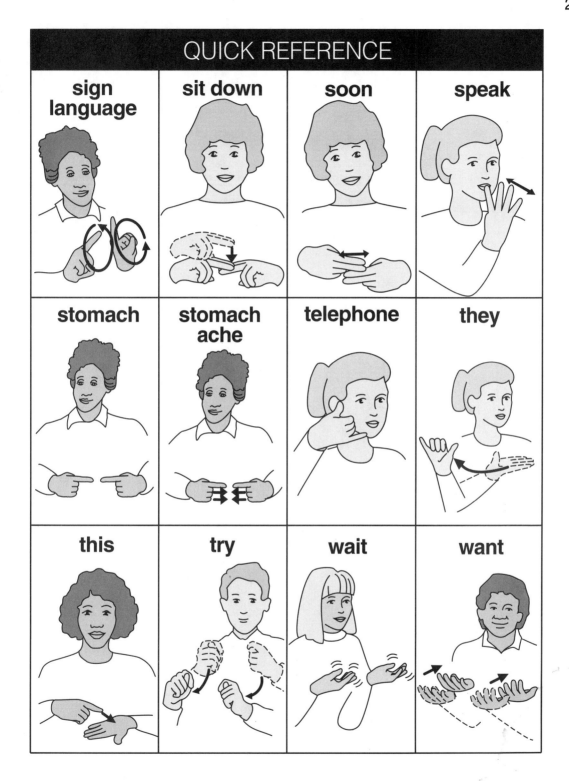

sign language	sit down	soon	speak
stomach	**stomach ache**	**telephone**	**they**
this	**try**	**wait**	**want**

QUICK REFERENCE

what	when	where	who
wife	with	x-ray	you
your			

Index

Also available from
Garlic Press

A Word in the Hand

GP-008

A Word in the Hand, Book 2

GP-040

Basic primers to Signed English, containing illustrations, lessons, exercises, and assignments.

Finger Alphabet Cards

GP-009

Sign Number Cards

GP-022

Sturdy 8 1/2" x 11" cards for the alphabet and numbers through 20.

Basic Sign Primer Cards

GP-036

Basic Sign Vocabulary, Set A

GP-023

Basic Sign Vocabulary, Set B

GP-024

Each set contains 100 basic vocabulary words with appropriate signs.

Sound Hearing

GP-026

Tape and booklet to demonstrate sound, hearing, and hearing loss.

Beginning Sign Language Series: The Finger Alphabet

GP-046

Beginning Sign Language Series: Signing at School

GP-047

Beginning Sign Language Series: Can I Help?

GP-057

Beginning Sign Language Series: Caring for Young Children

GP-058

Topical signing for beginning signers of all ages.